Praise for AC Benus
from the members of gayauthors.org

Witty, fast-moving, filled with a collection of colourful, eccentric, and somewhat questionable characters. Superbly written and thoroughly entertaining.
>—Dodger

Can I just say [Mojo] is akin to *Much Ado About Nothing* or some such Shakespeare play where everyone is double-crossing everyone, and there's so much sex and intrigue and comedy throughout that you don't know whether to gasp or groan or laugh as you read? Each sentence is purposeful and moves the story forward. Your characters sizzle with personalities
>—MacGreg

I do not know how to say this – every line AC writes sizzles with innuendo and hidden meaning. Each chapter is golden.
>—Will Hawkins

Iced-tea glass raised, I want to toast AC for his untiring efforts – or maybe persistent efforts despite fatigue – to entertain and engage us in every scene.
>—knotme

This story is great! I couldn't stop reading. The main characters are very vivid and lovable for all their faults
>—Lyssa

Oh, my . . . this writing is incredible . . . it sweeps me away and I am in that place and with those characters. Each chapter is no different: 1,000 words or 10,000, it's never enough.
>—Mikiesboy

It's so fun to read an actually witty story with brains behind it; it perks up my evenings.
>—Puppilull

Praise for AC Benus
from the members of gayauthors.org

"You positively insist your readers read between the lines." That is how I often feel as a reader of your work, AC. But is it stimulating rather than daunting, and very, very rewarding!
—J. Hunter Dunn

This has been an absolutely marvelous tale from beginning to end. You did it perfectly . . . *Bravissimo, maestro.*
—Parker Owens

What an interesting bunch AC has introduced us to. They are, by turns, over-sexed, under-sexed, scared, and funny. It's like that old movie *It's a Mad, Mad, Mad, Mad World* trying to keep up with who's doing what to whom!
—Mollyhousemouse

Two bananas, a hard-boiled egg, Eleanor Roosevelt, two Gay sailors, a Second World War Luger and some hot spanking. How's that for a writing prompt! This is turning into a masterpiece. No one can ever accuse AC of being predictable.
—Dodger

This is a wonderful book . . . Irreverent, naughty, brilliant, hysterical, and downright entertaining. Thanks a million times for writing it.
—Mikiesboy

You cannot help but be drawn into this wonderfully written story. The characters are vivid and come alive within AC's beautifully described locations. You can see it all in the words he chooses to paint with . . . . First class writing and entertainment
—MichaelS36

Be still, my heart! What a chase scene! What a confrontation . . . Just how many scenes can be sent up? This was like watching a firework show, one spectacular burst after another . . . I was breathless by the end. But I still wanted more.
—Parker Owens

Poetry Available from AC Benus

Hymenaios, or The Marriage of the God of Marriage
A Classical style myth in 2,600 lines of Blank Verse
ebook: ISBN 9781953389091; paperback: ISBN 9781953389084

Summer 2020 – Hell in a Handbasket
A contender for the Pulitzer Prize in poetry, 2021, this collection grapples with the year of pandemic, racial injustice and environmental crisis
ebook: ISBN 9781953389015; paperback: ISBN 9781953389008

The Thousandth Regiment
A Translation of and Commentary on Hans Ehrenbaum-Degele's First World War Poems "Das tausendste Regiment"
ebook: ISBN 1657220583; paperback: ISBN 9781657220584

A Man in a Room, and other poems
Verse following the year when the poet was 21 years old
ebook: ISBN 97817345103; paperback: ISBN 978173456107

The Easiest Thing in the World, and other poems
Marking the third anniversary of the Pulse Nightclub terror attack
ebook: ISBN 9781734561029; paperback: ISBN 9781734561036

Rima Fragmenta, or Fragments of a Rift
Fifty Sonnet for Kevin
ebook: ISBN 9781734561005; paperback: ISBN 9781734561012

First Love: Poems for Ross
For everyone's first love; both bitter and sweet
ebook: ISBN 9781734561081; paperback: ISBN 9781734561098

Poetry Available from AC Benus

Demon Dream
Redemption and shared humanity shine in this retelling of a medieval Japanese legend
    ebook: ISBN 9781953389138; paperback: ISBN 9781953389145

Audre Lorde Knows What I Mean – 2021 in Review
A follow-up to Summer 2020, *this collection grapples with the year of the Gop-led Capitol insurrection, racial injustice and the death throes of the environment*
    ebook: ISBN 9781953389015; paperback: ISBN 9781953389008

Mikhail Kraminsky, and other poems
Two collections of early poems exploring the pain of youth and being closeted
    ebook: ISBN 9781953389152; paperback: ISBN 9781953389169

One Hundred and Fifty-Five Sonnets for Tony
A bold testament to love
    ebook: ISBN 9781953389114; paperback: ISBN 9781953389107;
    hardback: ISBN 9781953389121

Love Looked at Me and Laughed – Poems for Brian
Love is not always easy. Poems to/for/about my first boyfriend
    ebook: ISBN 9781953389237; paperback: ISBN 9781953389220
    hardback: ISBN 978-1-953389-24-4

Love is Love (Contributor)
Poetry Anthology: In aid of Orlando's Pulse victims and survivors, Lily G. Blunt, Editor, 2016
        ebook: ISBN 153514369X; paperback: ISBN 153514369X

1940, 1970 & TODAY

PLUS OTHER POEMS

AC Benus

an AC Benus Impression
San Francisco

Grateful acknowledgement is here offered
for the support and encouragement
I've received on the literary site
www.gayauthors.org.

ISBN 978-1-953389-40-4 (ebook)
ISBN 978-1-953389-39-8 (paperback)

1940, 1970 AND TODAY:
PLUS OTHER POEMS.
Copyright © 2023 by AC Benus.

Library of Congress Control Number: 2023912951

CONTENTS

1940, 1970 and Today   13.

Endnotes   53.

1940, 1970
& TODAY

Poem No. 1 [1]

Kei

Nineteen he is. And young in what it mean to be a
nineteen-year-old Japanese boy. He eats prolifically,
laughs profoundly, finds mirrors in objects that reflect.
But his eyes sparkle beyond a culture or an age. In that
immensity does this indefinite sorrow live as only we can feel it
move beneath our own eyes. That flow of passion that can
produce for nature so little, but has made for mankind
nearly all its worth.

I on one line, he to another, by the divide must
we part. On the steps to go did he look at me, and then
I understood a sorrow too great to ever know. That
Connection made, the parting grew ever more impossible.
Nineteen and beautiful in his youth, he said a truth to me.

Poem No. 2 [2]
A Valentine for Kei

Sonnet:

I think of the poverty here encrypt,
Sighing for those who could love you better,
Then I give vicious thought to bolder script,
Which though slow, still has ways to unfetter.
Last night in my arms, my eyes beheld you –
Lashed down as you were by the charms of day –
But at least my hands knew just what to do
As conniving morning sought you away.
Asleep always nearer the ground's pyre,
I invoke the love that never is gone
With the sun of men; His phoenix-fire
Burns in the turtle's eyes, doomlessly on.

    Yet, as the morning bids you not to stay,
      The night shall bring you back;
    Then these eyes, my heart and hands won't defray
      The passions that I lack!

Poem No. 3 [3]
Also for Kei

All the faces on my floor
who make a bed of there and watch
the antics of a queer
move above them to a rhythm
that only he handles dear
brings him ever down.

Beneath the want of you
his desire for encore
when with you one part is through
the others under, list lines of more.

Poem No. 4

These are the days of which
   the ancients tell with
      boney fingers from their graves

Poem No. 5

朝の使者
愛後ろにあがる
とその耳にささやく
この愛の夢を
この愛起きる。

Messenger of the morn,
Ascend behind my love
And whisper in that ear
This love's dream;
Rouses this love of mine.

Poem No. 6

Prelude:

What could fall to me, not already mine?

How, before Pentecost, his followers stumbled,
saw darkness through the bright of day,
put fear in every dull corner
that it fathom their timorous glance,
that, with one voice, would call them out
for all the world to shame alike.

How they waited in fear
with groanings unutterable,
inapt for the date uncertain
when confidence becomes the coward
not even to death, but gives
reason to sorrow, skill to expression,
purpose to longing, and
action to love.

But what befell them, not already theirs?

Poem:
  Two Psalms

Lord, make me one of mind and memory
blind all that sees not love
stomp all in me
that might spread contempt.

Lord grant me recall every subtle form
of how my apathy did hate
when nothing made contempt its better;
that I remember I had eyes
but no soul to see;
hands to make
but not heart to create.

Lord, make me one with now and then
that every careless hurt I gave
returns to the truth about me.
Make me one with the hate I had
that love might make me whole again.

Make me one of mind and memory.

    o   o   o

Rend all from me that is
        not love;
that sees not love, that thinks not,
that feels not, in all that is.

A year or two goes by
and growth is nearly threatened
by the strategy of an absent mind;
this struggle finds me yet tonight,
though in this I take solace.

Divide away again and again
all that makes me not but one;
in the void of what I was,
contract to build its better
with these simple terms.

Rend all from me that is
        not love;
that sees not love, that thinks not,
that finds not, in all that is.

Poem No. 7 [4]

It was one of the rare times of man
    the devil was dead,
    and hope lay dancing in the streets;
    optimism in every bed.

But in the time evil was unimaginable
    it lived well and
    found form evenly in
    subtle features.

Poem No. 8

Too young to feel so old
too old to be so young
Without hope I'm neither
living nor wanting
yet now all I want
is to believe again
that life is more than hope
more than a heart . . . beat
Too young to have no soul
too old to faith me one unique

Poem No. 9

My passion has hands and eyes
and lines like desire

But how easily a minute of rain
or an afternoon of sun
could destroy this love of mine

How could it burn through in a moment
of absentminded neglect?

Poem No. 10

For Shakespeare's metre do we all sigh;
to believe like fact he'll but ride the wave
beyond us all, and W. H. will not die
as long as lips can move him out of his grave.

Poem No. 11 [5]

Here we sit today at summer's end,
On the advantageous side of despair.

Poem No. 12 [6]

Arrival at 9:30

Haibun:

Nothing happened till 12:15 when Etchan wanted to get cigarettes. Instead we found a Tunisian guy who invited us to his birthday party, which was the following day. Also, she started talking to the French guy who was leaving, and who had sat in front and to the left of us. On the right side was some nice looking guy, but endowed with the personality of an ass-aperture. He was with a Japanese guy (at whom he blew smoke, in his eyes). I talked to him finally when he sat next to me. His name is Hiko (a nickname) from Kyoto, who sometimes comes to Tokyo for a getaway, and was staying with the asshole. I guess Hiko likes him; if he let his eyes guide his choice, I would agree, but what a vain and worthless soul the object of his ardor has. What a shame for any affection the Japanese boy expends on him.

I don't want to forget his eyes
the way he held his lover's hand
his shoeless socks, his shining face
the smile that it became for me.
I don't want to forget his eyes
or the way he abashed when
I whispered how lovely
To me I think they are.
His hand drew me near
a gentle pull on my thigh,
four hands held together,
sweet looks passed,
and I with concern
saw how sad a moment
two-yet-one can share . . .
But as it passed, so
might this. Yet,
I don't want to forget his eyes.

◇ ◇ ◇

Poem No. 13

Love like sleep
numbing still so
that I can hardly
hold this pen to purpose

how do I want you
how many times must I ask
if stealing into slumber can't
relieve this wont of sleep

drone and drone some more
one minute in your arms
the next free, but free to what?
Love like sleep, I want you so.

Urbanity fails when nothing
but desire is all I hold
to compare empty night
with the nothing of empty night –
but never is it so in reverse.

Poem No. 14 [7]

Boy with the beautiful eyebrows
Take your lovely sad eyes burrowed beneath
And with them look at me.

Sweet sad-sighted boy
Up-turn your head from the floor
And look at me that I
Might smile away that ever-sweetening
Sorrow and caress those beautiful brows

Boy with the beautiful eyebrows
Take those sad eyes furrowed underneath
And look at me.

Poem No. 15 [8]

1940,1970 and Today

Poem:

What if I were one of them,
one of the ones bound in a line –
on one side held by oppression,
on the stronger side still, by a fact –
bound because they couldn't hide
what others easily scurry into themselves.
With shaven heads wrapped
in soil and sweat-combed rags,
the line without a sound conjoins
into a row of wasted solitude,
looking all calm, but beneath
a bitter quake of the heart.

One palm sweats where
its own nails bite,
longing for sweet revolt,
or just a little courage to touch
the mate it used to hold
so often and so well.
More spitefully, the living barbs
cut his flesh, bringing blood
to the face of constraint;
sweat and purity mingle
in the cupping want of his hand.
Fear, alive within reach, his eyes
feel sunken deeper in his brain,
but focus worked by weariness
brings an image to attention.
That head before his groping eyes
he sees as summers ago have seen –
where the back of ears were
once awash in sun-like hair –
he would play like a child
on a familiar beach,
stroke a fingertip from nape
around to the side of receiving lobe,

then like a dalliance, retread the way
to end in the sandy spot from which he began.
Letting go, his eyes befell the faded stripes
that downwards clothed the back before him,
and beneath, the shabby remains
of a body he used to feel his own.
Down to himself, his own badge –
the one they gave him as a shame –
he sees the pink triangle gone a dirty
emaciated hue of the time stolen from him.
But movement from in front
caught his ever-slowing glance,
and a blink required a second
to clear his vision,
but movement he saw
from the hand of he in front of him –
from the one he so longed to touch.
Perhaps not an invitation,
perhaps merely a glint
of movement hoping
across a blind desert
for the embrace of a loving eye.
Three sides, the man mused.

Half empty-hearted,
one side denies;
and if unfeeling can
deny a life away,
a second side is shame
to only be alive when
more than one, for
a group in uncurable
illness is a group in
pathetic penitence strong.
But the third and last
is redemption, the one
so few seem to find;
the acquittal of nature,
the strength to free her
of any wrong,
and that love of self
is the only love
to bring about
blessèd absolution.
The man's grip relaxed,
and the nails undug
their trench from his palm.

With one finger slowly raising,
his eyes re-found that
distant glimmer, and made for it
across the dead air of
time robbed from them.
Slowly, for the effort took much . . .
slowly, no one must see,
no one must, not for shame,
not for grief, but for no other
reason than a secret love
ever wants its innocence.
Again he woke his eyes to focus,
only to feel the palm of his belovèd
take the finger in affection.
A moment only, but neither needed more.
quickly, he drew his hand away
and then saw a guard
had seen their touch.
To the man, the soldier boy
was familiar – the same sweet look
he knew so well – the look his lover
used to wear so mildly
and so openly in the Berlin of old.

A lump hitched in his throat;
not only had this boy seen,
but he was one of them;
one of them hidden and helpless.
The man had no illusions;
such types were the most deadly
to his type – the caught,
the unapologetic, the "uncured,"
and the natural . . . .
He feared the worst. He felt
sorry it meant the same pain
for his belovèd as himself,
wishing he could absorb it
for the man he loved.
A flinch of pity appeared
across the young face;
the guard moved silently away.
Eventually, the order came
and the line of men
trudged forward at a shuffling pace,
their last movement, for
outside the camp gates,
a ditch awaited them.

So the order was brought about
against those – the accusèd Queers –
by the un-accusèd ones
in a place called Belsen.

◇ ◇ ◇

But what if I were one of them,
the trickle in the streets who,
by the end of morning,
thousands found themselves.
One of the ones who joined
autonomous limbs and built
an unhanded chain to sweep
arbitrary subjugation aside.
One who reveled in the
sheer weight of all my companions,
we being one, we taking
power so long denied.
Alive in the joy of freedom,
itching for the chance to fight –
whole, happy, strong –
with the strength
of newborns.

What if I were one of them,
the ones who matched on
a bright summer day –
one year to the day –
after Stonewall.
What if I were amongst
the first takers of the
Rights of Queers!

◇ ◇ ◇

Postlude:
Sonnet

But those generations are gone for me,
Though less than one divides the former from
The one that got all of our liberty;
Thirty-year rebellion from martyrdom.
And yet today among the crowd I saw
Beauty has eyes and hands, and kept below
Levi's brand, are treasures near the draw,
Handy enough to keep me in sorrow.

Moving like one beyond their concerning,
A boy saw and shyly knew the compliment –
As shadows blew me his glance returning,
Our commonest love with the crowd's was blent.
    Though such days are past, those they loved I see;
    I'll fight that these years belong to him and me!

Poem No. 16

A Final Verse
closing out a poetic notebook

Of all the things a man could love
    – in the world wide and green –
Or conceived in all the spheres above,
      to love a man, is the best between!

Poem No. 17

The more power I get
the more I want the worthless
age of my youth to return.

Poem No. 18 [9]

As I walk in the rain,
a girl sways in front of me.
Her big blue *kasa*
shows me flashes of hair,
her ivory-sweatered back,
her left hand swinging freely,
hips rocking mini-skirted legs.
A boy comes out of a shop in front of her,
deftly crosses the narrow street's other side,
and falls in line between me and the girl.
The water gently taps his short-cropped hair,
his red bomber jacket –
white letters scripted across the back –
his pants of tan denim,
and one hand in his pocket.

As I walk in the rain,
behind the both of them,
I can see him glance at the girl,
Not knowing I know
He wants her
And that
I want him.

Poem No. 19 [10]

quote in a letter to Joseph Blass,
attributed to Shakespeare

"What could be the odds, minds over the miles
Might meet each other in the same idea."

Poem No. 20

"Some say fire, some say ice" –
but they're not fooling me any.
I know the world's damning price
will be exacted to the penny
through a marketing device.

Poem No. 21

How sweet the hard sunshine scents
the softer things below it.

Poem No. 22

We architects of the West
have to exorcize our Classical demon,
or simply learn to exercise him better.

Poem No. 23

Every word writes
'More alone than before.'

Poem No. 24

Pen and paper,
white-clad forelegs
and the eyes of a poet.

"Not beauty. Not again," he thought.
"That word comes back
"every time my soul seems stirred;
"Not this time." He looked up
because he was being looked at.
An average man, a black-double-breast,
turned his eyes away.
"Cute enough," he thought
and wrote; the first line now
joined by a second, then
by a third.

> 'Today the train swells,
> the every-bodies and them
> placed in seats around . . . '

He glanced up. The black-jacket
glanced back, but his eyes,
to the other's surprise, looked not at him
but what rested on a notebook
there on his thighs.

Pen and paper,
white jeans, shaved head,
he caught me looking at him.
A young man, beautiful, living
on the train that carted all of us,
the far-more dead, back and forth
to our pseudo lives.

"Not beauty, not again," he thought,
but his song would not be sung
without it. Let me finish it for him.

Poem No. 25

    Tanka:

Two boys on bikes are
Calling 'bye' out on the street;
Through autumn twilight
Their voices call like waved hands,
Never doubting reunion.

Poem No. 26

    Tanka:

An empty mailbox,
A machine that's unanswered;
These are the hard ones
At day's end to overcome,
These small everyday sorrows.

Poem No. 27

Yet wanting more than passion
One part of wisdom could fall down to me
One that sets the fashion
When it dances to set all of us free.

        One part saying other parts to me.

Poem No. 28

Tanka:

Sitting on his arms
A man holds his sleeping son,
Never suspecting
The boy breathing on his neck
Takes future memories of him.

Poem No. 29

Give me a boy who walks in beauty,
And all the rest will follow.

Poem No. 30

Yet the heart retreats to a hunger bold,
And old woes will sometimes new wails decry,
Not letting new grief luxury in old
As hope can oft better senses deny.

Poem No. 31
. . . On seeing a Satsuma Vase . . .

Tanka:

Filtering from there,
Heaven's sun shines light down, while,
Under this spring day,
An unpeaceful heart follows
The blossoms' bloom, ebb and fall.

Poem No. 32

Love is the only excuse
Worth excusing.

Poem No. 33 [11]
A Joke Tanka

Tanka:

Sleepy in my work,
Caked mucus falls from my lids
Down to the paper
Where a day of me was lost
To ink and love-less action.

Poem No. 34 [12]

Tanka:

Boys on the Tama,
Some in tank tops, some shirtless;
Wind-shaped clouds above,
And a rushing train with me
Somewhere lost in the middle.

Poem No. 35

"To a Boy on a July Saturday"
concurrent with my reading of Plato's Theaetetus

For just a moment seen –
a boy of real beauty
who studies alone

Sits like a god unknown –
among the sea of us
mediocrity.

The train goes noisily on around him,
but those eyes search over the faces,
not for a glimpse of their hopes or dreams,
but wanders to-and-fro to find out
the physics equations
he slowly puts to memory.

But there alive is he –
a little smile for
a code remembered

And the little smile –
he doesn't know I've seen;
doesn't know it moves.

The train goes noisily on around him.
a perfect place for him to be alone,
unknowing the grace his eyes and lips
show the world all hard and unseeing;
but, there alive is he,
and not so in the car, but in me.

Eyes sincere and sweetly kind –
that will never seek me out
I'll bring to other times

For such beauty as yours –
is want in the lesser
moments of my life.

Poem No. 36 [13]

Tanka:

The first moment down
Amid the squeal of the bar;
But dark and quiet,
All eyes fall to Hubert's arms,
While he looks only at me.

Poem No. 37

The less oppressed are we,
The greater we rise
To the occasion of
Our liberty.

Poem No. 38

There is no beauty like
    that of man himself;
    no god his better,
    no devil his equal.

(Original, crossed-out version:)

    There is no beauty
like unto man himself;
    no god as powerful,
    no devil as accountable.

Poem No. 39 [14]

Tanka:

In the street or train,
The smell of autumn's peaches
Finds me still and rich,
To remind me life, like they,
Fall swift as *kinmokusei*.

~

1940, 1970 & TODAY

Endnotes

Endnotes:

[1] "Kei" The poems presented in this book cover the years of composition 1992, 1993 and 1994. This excludes poems specifically collected in previously published volumes, like the respective sets for Jimmy and Sunny.

What's recorded in this book are scenes from long ago now, and with this opening poem, I recovered through editing it that the "line" reference refers to train lines. Kei and I met one night in late January 1992, and wound up closing the bar. As we trundled off to catch our respective last trains, Kei assisted a homeless man carry his cart down the steps of Shinjuku station. His kindness – explaining to me that he'd noticed the man's leg was injured – made a profound impression on me. Later, in the nearly empty station, he kissed me before we parted to head to our platforms. But, once we got up to them, we could see one another and continued to interact in a silent, touching way. No one else was around, and something clicked in both of us. We called each other the next day and got together, although we did not sleep with one another until February 13th, as hinted in the next poem.

[2] "A Valentine for Kei" Dated February 14th, 1992, this poem's mention of a phoenix and turtle alludes to what is reputed to be Shakespeare's final love poem for Mr. W. H. – the *onlie* recipient of the 154 *W. H. Sonnets,* published in 1609, in the poet's lifetime. Here is an extract from the conclusion of *The Phoenix and Turtle:*

> Beauty, truth, and rarity,
> Grace in all simplicity,
> Here enclosed in cinders lie.
>
> Death is now the phoenix' nest;
> And the turtle's loyal breast
> To eternity doth rest.

(quoted from *William Shakespeare: The Complete Works* [Arthur Henry Bullen, Editor] (Stratford-upon-Avon 1904), p. 1252)

[3] "Also for Kei" The floor references in this poem (and the previous two) are fairly literal, as my apartment in the Kichijohji section of Tokyo was so small, I used a pair of *futon* for bedding. Traditional futon are foldable mattresses stashed in dedicated cupboards during the day. Part of the ritual of going to bed involves arranging the futons and pillows, the covers and comforters, for the night.

[4] "Arrival at 9:30" The events captured in this poem are related to those portrayed in my first novel *The Round People.*

Also related to the fictionalized environment captured in the novel is a collection of love poetry. It was written for a boy I met in the real-life setting which inspired the book. He was a Japanese guy, only a couple years younger than I, and whom everyone knew as Jimmy. We met while he was bartending at this 'gaijin bar' – which means a weekday watering hole for locals and a weekend-desti-nation dance club. It catered to international residents of the city and those Japanese folks who wished to socialize with them. This club, named *De-Ja-Vu,* was in my neighborhood of Tokyo. Jimmy and I became friends, and although straight, I came out to him. A mutual friend of ours had already revealed my feelings for the handsome young man, and this revelation seemed to only make us closer.

The Round People may be found in its entirety here:

https://gayauthors.org/story/ac
-benus/theroundpeople-
anovel/

Sweetest Grief to Hold, the collection of love poetry for Jimmy, may be found in the book titled *After Days of Rain and other poems: from my twenty-third year:*

https://gayauthors.org/story/ac
-benus/after-days-of-rain-and-

[5] "It was one of the rare times of Man" This poem speaks to the time after the crackdown in Tiananmen Square (June 1989), then the fall of the Berlin Wall (December 1989), and the eventual change in Russia from one-party rule to a democracy (December 1991). In retrospect, looking back on when it was written in 1992, the darker forecast of the poem's proved quite prophetic. Now America is faced with the terror of one-party rule by the Gops (2015), who, with the help of totalitarian Russia and the People's (so-called) Army of red China, have brought waterboarding to George Washington's army (2001) and January 6th to the nation's Capitol (2021).

[6] "Here we sit today at summer's end" The idea contained in Poem No. 11 was utilized and expanded in the sixth *Becoming Real* short story ("In Six Hours"), which I was writing at the time.

[7] "Boy with the beautiful eyebrows" This poem represents a vignette inspired by daily commutes on trains in Tokyo. On such trips, one spies the most interesting sights (and guys).

[8] "1940, 1970 and Today" This poem, contrasting the Nazi extermination of Gay people with the 1st anniversary Pride March to commemorate the Stonewall freedom riots, was inspired by my reading of a little book I bought in the college bookstore of Ochanomizu, Tokyo. My first books on LGBTI2S+ *belle lettres* came from here, and began a process of eye-opening to the extent of Queer History which continues to this day. The little book in question is an analysis of the 1979 play *Bent.*

What is less evident – *1940, 1970 and Today* – is that "today" refers to the 1993 LGBT March on Washington. Over a million people gathered that momentous day on the National Mall, demanding equal rights, and caused instant Gay-erasing from D.C. police. They, despite all the arial photographic proof of the million or more present, lied and offered a laughable *official count* – the one that goes into the history books – of "under 50 thousand." It was the powers-that-be's way to slap the Gay Community in the face and reinforce that Queer lives do not matter; they're not even important enough to count, literally. Just like Trump and his so-called census-taking in the year 2020. If you believe that BS, our minority group "shrunk" over ten years, notwithstanding all actual facts to the contrary.

Ironically, despite the proof that millions of Gay people were killed by the Nazis because of their orientation, an "official" tally – the one all the politicians use even to this day to marginalize our Holocaust experience

– stands at less than 50,000.

[9] "As I walk in the rain" *Kasa* is the Japanese word for umbrella.

I still remember the circumstances of this poem: the wet day; coming out of the Seiyu in Fujimigaoka with groceries; seeing the pair of people walking ahead of me . . . . Poems are great time machines.

[10] "What could be the odds" Joseph Blass was a Lebanese-Québécois friend of mine in Tokyo. This Montreal native left not too long after we met, and I remember his next stop was Russia's far east. He sent me letters from his voyage on the Trans-Siberian Railway, while reading Dosto-evsky's *Brothers Karamazov,* which he raved about. Although decades ago now, he's still one ahead of me, as I've yet to read it. But Joe's glowing reviews have always stayed with me, as well as his sweet, accommo-datingly patient ways with me when we dated.

[11] "A Joke Tanka" The March 22, 1994, original of this poem contains the following explanatory note:

Not that I worked without love for my work, but that the day was spent on it and not in the company of the people I loved.

[12] "Boys on the Tama" The Tama River, which forms the southern border for the City of Tokyo, has a broad channel for when the river floods. Most times of the year, this area serves as wide-open parkland. Passing over the river on my daily train, I began to envy the freedom and camara-derie of the young men exercising down along the riverbanks.

[13] "The first moment down" Hubert was a bartender at Arty-Farty, a foreigner-friendly bar and dance club in Tokyo's Gay neighborhood, Shinjuku Ni-Chome [pronounced *Knee-Cho'may*]. From Hong Kong, he cut a striking figure. Tall, handsome, slightly cross-eyed, he spent much time at the gym honing his impeccably sculpted arms, the upper parts of which he showcased by only wearing muscleman Ts when he worked. We'd sometimes go have coffee on his breaks, or something stronger after the bars closed at 2 a.m.

[14] "In the street or on the train" The *kinmokusei* (金木犀) referenced is to the plant *Osmanthus fragrans.* The orange blossoms of this smaller-sized tree appear in October with the most enchanting scent imaginable.

www.ingramcontent.com/pod-product-compliance
Lightning Source LLC
LaVergne TN
LVHW041209080426
835508LV00008B/864

9 781953 389398